THIS LAND CALLED AMERICA: OHIO

CREATIVE EDUCATION

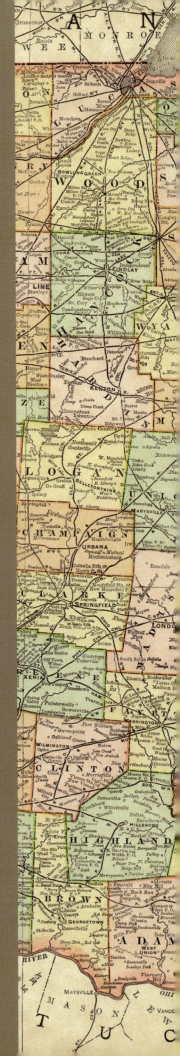

Published by Creative Education

P.O. Box 227, Mankato, Minnesota 56002

Creative Education is an imprint of The Creative Company

www.thecreativecompany.us

Design by Blue Design (www.bluedes.com)

Art direction by Rita Marshall

Book production by The Design Lab

Printed in the United States of America

Photographs by Alamy (dmac, Greenshoots Communications, Lebrecht Music
and Arts Photo Library, William Manning, North Wind Picture Archives, Rene
Paik, James Quine, Tom Till), Corbis (Bettmann, Layne Kennedy, Michael
Masian Historic Photographs, Bob Rowan/Progressive Image), Dreamstime
(Glitterd), Getty Images (Cincinnati Museum Center, Andreas Feininger//
Time & Life Pictures, Bruce Forster, Hulton Archive, Francis Miller//Time
& Life Pictures, Charles Peterson, Jim Rogash, Robert Postma), iStockphoto
(Diana Lundin, Ken Love)

Library of Congress Cataloging-in-Publication Data

Gunderson, Jessica.

Ohio / by Jessica Gunderson.

p. cm. — (This land called America)

Includes bibliographical references and index.

ISBN 978-1-58341-788-1

1. Ohio—Juvenile literature. I. Title. II. Series.

F491.3.G86 2009

977.1—dc22   200800951

First Edition

9 8 7 6 5 4 3 2 1

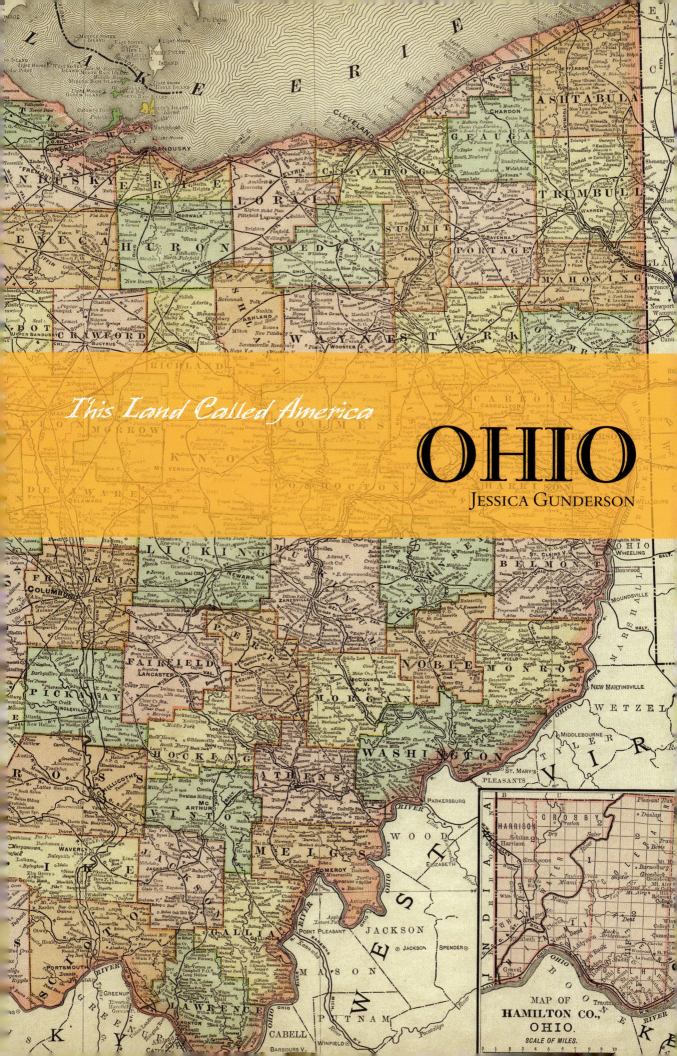

This Land Called America

OHIO

Jessica Gunderson

Ohio

JESSICA GUNDERSON

A SHIP'S CAPTAIN WAVES TO THE CROWDS
ON THE DOCKS AS THE SHIP SETS SAIL. STEEL,
COAL, AND RUBBER ARE STORED IN THE
SHIP'S CARGO HOLD. OTHER SHIPS IN THE
GLISTENING WATERS OF LAKE ERIE ALSO CARRY
GOODS MADE IN OHIO. ON THE SHORELINE,
SKYSCRAPERS AND FACTORIES REACH TOWARD
THE CLOUDS. NOT FAR OFF, FORESTS SKIRT THE
SKY. RIVERS AND CANALS FLOW TOWARD THE
LAKE. THESE WATERWAYS ARE THE LIFELINE OF
THE STATE. THE SHIP WILL CARRY ITS GOODS
TO FAR-OFF PLACES, BUT IT WILL SOON RETURN
TO OHIO, A LAND OF INDUSTRY, WATER, AND
INCREDIBLE BEAUTY.

YEAR	EVENT
1669	Frenchman René-Robert de La Salle is the first European to explore Ohio.

Gateway to the West

Two thousand years ago, the ancient Mound Builders lived in the land that would one day become Ohio. They were the first to farm the land, and they traded their goods with other ancient people far and wide. Later, American Indian tribes such as the Delaware, Shawnee, Miami, and Wyandot moved into

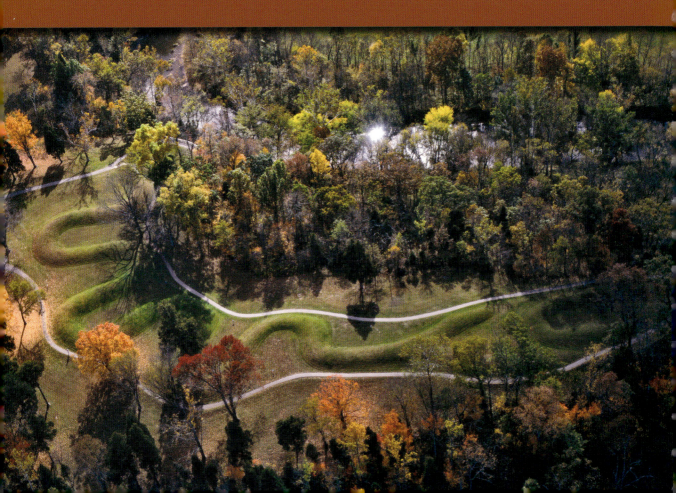

the area from other parts of North America. Like the Mound Builders, these tribes farmed, fished, and hunted.

Around the year 1669, French explorer René-Robert de La Salle became the first European to set foot in Ohio. Because of La Salle's travels, France claimed the Ohio region. At the same time, English settlers were moving into the area. Both countries wanted control of Ohio and the surrounding land. A war between France and England began in 1754. Nine years later, France surrendered and signed the land over to England.

Not long after the war between France and England ended, the Revolutionary War broke out between England and the 13

When white settlers moved to Ohio, they built mission churches to convert Indians to Christianity.

The Mound Builders' 1,330-foot-long (405 m) Serpent Mound looks like an uncoiling snake.

YEAR

1763 The French and Indian War ends, and France gives Ohio to England.

EVENT

- 7 -

U.S. soldiers battled against Ohio's natives during the 1790s so that other people could settle there.

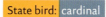
State bird: cardinal

Battle of Fallen Timbers

American colonies on the East Coast. The colonists wished to be free of English rule. America won the war in 1783, and Ohio became an American territory. More white settlers soon moved there.

For a few years, the settlers and the American Indian tribes lived together peacefully. But by 1791, any friendship between the two groups had faded. The Indians feared they would be forced from their land, and battles erupted throughout Ohio. After years of fighting, the Indians signed a peace agreement called a treaty in 1795. The treaty gave much of Ohio to the United States. The Indians were forced to move to lands called reservations that were set aside for them. Most Indian reservations were far from Ohio.

The rich soil of Ohio drew many more settlers, and on March 1, 1803, Ohio became America's 17th state. Many settlers made their living by farming. Their crops were so plentiful that they had much to sell. But it was difficult to haul goods across the land. In 1825, construction began on water canals across Ohio. The canals linked major rivers. Farmers could use the canals to carry their goods by boat, which was much faster.

Railroads also appeared in Ohio in the early 1800s. By 1860, railroads connected Ohio to most major American

YEAR
1788   Ohio's first permanent settlement, Marietta, is established by General Rufus Putnam.
EVENT

- *9* -

John D. Rockefeller made a fortune from the oil business, becoming the first American billionaire.

cities. Because travelers heading west could easily reach Ohio from many places in the country, Ohio was briefly nicknamed "The Gateway to the West."

Another important railroad was operating in Ohio during this time. It was called the Underground Railroad. The Underground Railroad was not a real railroad. It was a string of hiding places for runaway slaves. Slaves from the South traveled on the Underground Railroad north to Canada, where they would be free. Many Ohioans helped runaways escape slavery by hiding them in their attics, cellars, and barns. When the Civil War broke out in 1861, Ohio sided with the Northern, anti-slavery states.

In 1870, a man named John D. Rockefeller started an oil business in Cleveland called the Standard Oil Company. It became one of the world's largest companies. Steel mills, tire factories, and glass factories also soon sprang up throughout Ohio. Ohio's location near Lake Erie and other waterways made manufactured goods easy to transport. By the turn of the century, Ohio had shifted from a farming state to an industrial one.

Railway transportation became increasingly important in Ohio throughout the early 1900s.

YEAR

1803

Ohio becomes the 17th state on March 1, with Chillicothe serving as its capital until 1810.

EVENT

Beautiful Water

Ohio is a Great Lakes state on the eastern edge of the Midwest. It is bordered by Lake Erie on the north. On the other side of the lake is the country of Canada. Pennsylvania and West Virginia border Ohio on the east. To the south is Kentucky, to the west is Indiana, and to the northwest is Michigan.

The name Ohio is taken from an Iroquois Indian word meaning "great river." Ohio has many great rivers, such as the Cuyahoga River, which flows north into Lake Erie. The Ohio River runs along Ohio's southern border. The state's landscape is sprinkled with smaller rivers, canals, and lakes as well.

Lake Erie is the most important lake in Ohio. Its shoreline extends across 312 miles (502 km) of Ohio's bluffs and beaches. It provides the means to ship many of the state's manufactured goods. Lake Erie also has many beaches and islands, providing recreation for Ohio residents and visitors.

Ohio's land is rich and diverse, with lush forests, fertile farmland, and plentiful deposits of coal, oil, limestone, and salt. There are four major geographical regions in Ohio: the Till Plains in the west, the Lake Plains in the north, the Appalachian Plateau in the east, and the Bluegrass Region at the southern tip.

Boat and barge traffic is steady on two of Ohio's major rivers, the Cuyahoga (opposite), in Cleveland, and the Ohio (above).

YEAR
1816   Columbus becomes the capital of Ohio.
EVENT

Amish farm

Ohio coal

T he Till Plains region produces many of Ohio's crops, such as soybeans and corn. In the north, the soil of the Lake Plains grows fruits and vegetables. Part of the Lake Plains region used to be covered by the Black Swamp. In the mid-1800s, settlers in the area drained the swamp. Today, the region has some of the best soil in the state.

The Appalachian Plateau is a hilly region in eastern and southern Ohio. Beneath the Appalachian Plateau lies a treasure trove of natural resources such as salt, oil, and coal. There is enough salt in Ohio to meet Americans' needs for thousands of years to come. Ohio's coal is mined by a technique known as strip mining. The top layers of the land are peeled away by heavy machinery. Beneath the layers of dirt are strips of coal. The coal is dug out and shipped to nearby power plants, where it is burned to make electricity.

Ohio supports a large Amish community, many of whom farm (above), and is home to a few mines (opposite) that remain from coal's 19th-century heyday.

YEAR

1832

EVENT

The Ohio & Erie Canal opens, linking the Ohio River with Lake Erie.

The red fox is found throughout much of North America, as its favorite habitats are wooded areas and prairies.

Between the Till Plains and the Appalachian Plateau lies the Bluegrass Region of southern Ohio. This region is small. It is characterized by gentle, rolling hills and green pastures.

When Europeans first arrived in Ohio, they found a land completely covered in forests. The land changed quickly as trees were chopped down to build and heat homes. Today, forests of oak, hickory, beech, and sycamore cover about one-fourth of the state. The buckeye, a small, nut-bearing tree, is also found throughout Ohio. The abundance of buckeyes caused the state to be nicknamed "The Buckeye State."

White-tailed deer thrive in Ohio's forests. Other wildlife in Ohio includes red foxes, muskrats, woodchucks, and opossums. Ohio's rivers and streams are thick with fish such as bass, pike, muskellunge, and perch.

The weather in Ohio is hot and humid during the summer and cold and dry during the winter. The state receives an average of 38 inches (97 cm) of precipitation a year. Ohio is on the eastern edge of the area of the country known as "Tornado Alley." Residents watch for tornadoes from April through July.

The Ohio buckeye is the state tree of Ohio and is primarily found throughout the Midwest.

YEAR
1869 The Cincinnati Red Stockings become the first professional baseball team in the country.
EVENT

People and Presidents

THE FIRST EUROPEANS WERE DRAWN TO OHIO BECAUSE OF ITS PLENTIFUL WILDLIFE. FUR TRADERS MADE A GOOD LIVING SELLING THE PELTS (OR FURS) OF BEAVERS, BEARS, WOLVES, AND MINKS. ONCE THE FUR TRADE DIED DOWN, THOUGH, OTHER SETTLERS CAME TO FARM.

Today, some Ohioans still farm for a living. Although the state has many large, corporate-owned farms, small family farms continue to thrive. Farmers grow soybeans, corn, and wheat. Some raise hogs, poultry, and cattle. About one in seven Ohioans work in agriculture-related jobs such as farming, food processing, and meat packing.

About 35 percent of Ohio's residents have careers in the service industry. They provide food, transportation, or banking services. Education is another area in which many Ohioans work. More than 24,000 people are employed at Columbus's Ohio State University alone.

Large turkey farms are found in northwestern Ohio between the cities of Toledo and Lima.

A 19th-century painting by John Casper Wild (opposite) gives an early view of Cincinnati's waterfront.

YEAR

1913   The Ohio River floods, destroying much of the city of Dayton and killing almost 430 people.

EVENT

The many factories along the Ohio River (opposite) produce goods and parts for industries such as steel manufacturing (right).

Many Ohioans work in the manufacturing industry, making soap, steel, tires, and other equipment and machines. General Electric, which produces electrical equipment, is the top manufacturer in the state. Although the auto industry also employs many Ohio residents, the greatest majority of the population works in retail for companies such as Wal-Mart.

Ohio has the 7th-largest population in the country, but it is 34th in size. That means that the land is densely populated, with about 256 people per square mile (2.6 sq km). More than three-fourths of Ohio's people live in large cities such as Columbus, Cleveland, and Cincinnati.

Most Ohioans are white. About 12 percent are African American. A small percentage of Ohio's population is Hispanic, Asian, or American Indian. About 55,000 Amish people live in Ohio. This is the largest Amish community in North America.

YEAR
1955   The Ohio Turnpike, a major toll road that runs from east to west across the state, opens.
EVENT

The Amish originally immigrated to the U.S. from Switzerland. They live simply, without cars or electricity. The Amish are not completely separate from other Ohioans, however. They make and sell furniture, quilts, and baked goods.

An illustration from Uncle Tom's Cabin shows the main character Tom reading to fellow slaves.

Ohio has produced many great people, some of whom have become national leaders. Ohio is often called "The Mother of Modern Presidents." Seven U.S. presidents were born in Ohio, which is more than any other state besides Virginia has produced. The Ohio presidents are Ulysses S. Grant, Rutherford B. Hayes, James A. Garfield, Benjamin Harrison, William McKinley, William Taft, and Warren G. Harding. They all served within a span of 54 years, from 1869 to 1923.

Equality and freedom have long been important to the people of Ohio. In 1852, a woman named Harriet Beecher Stowe wrote an important book called *Uncle Tom's Cabin*. The book told of the horrors of slavery and caused many Americans to want slavery to be banned. Stowe, who had lived in Cincinnati for much of her adult life, had helped fugitive slaves escape to freedom.

Amish buggies are a common sight along country roads in parts of eastern Ohio.

YEAR

1967   Carl Stokes becomes mayor of Cleveland, making him the first African American mayor of a major U.S. city.

EVENT

I n the 1930s, an African American jazz musician from Toledo named Art Tatum rose to fame. Despite being nearly blind, Tatum followed his love of music and became one of the most famous jazz pianists in the world. In 1967, Cleveland mayor Carl Stokes became the first African American mayor of a major U.S. city.

Ohio's Oberlin College was the first college in the U.S. to offer education to both men and women. Oberlin also allowed students of all races to attend. Wilberforce University was the first private American college dedicated to educating African Americans.

A prominent feature on the campus of Oberlin College, the Memorial Arch (opposite) was dedicated in 1903, six years before jazz pianist Art Tatum (above) was born.

1970   Four Kent State University students are killed by the National Guard while protesting against the Vietnam War.

Flying Colors

OHIO IS KNOWN AS THE BIRTHPLACE OF AVIATION. IN 1903, TWO BROTHERS FROM OHIO, WILBUR AND ORVILLE WRIGHT, BUILT THE WORLD'S FIRST AIRPLANE. FAMOUS ASTRONAUTS JOHN GLENN AND NEIL ARMSTRONG WERE FROM OHIO AS WELL. THE OHIO QUARTER, RELEASED IN 2002, CELEBRATES THE FAMOUS FLIERS. ON THE BACK OF THE QUARTER IS AN ENGRAVING OF AN ASTRONAUT

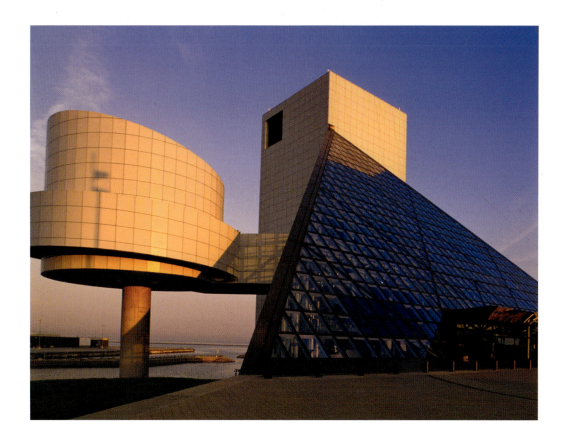

and the first airplane, along with the words "Birthplace of Aviation Pioneers." At the U.S. Air Force Museum in Dayton, flight enthusiasts can view World War II bombers and an Apollo space capsule.

Cleveland's Rock and Roll Hall of Fame building was designed by famous architect I. M. Pei.

Music lovers also have something to see in Ohio. Cleveland is home to the Rock and Roll Hall of Fame and Museum. Opened in 1995, the Hall of Fame adds important rock stars each year. The museum displays memorabilia from different eras in rock-and-roll history.

Just south of Cleveland, another hall of fame attracts visitors. The Pro Football Hall of Fame is located in Canton, Ohio. Visitors can see jerseys, footballs, and bronze busts of every player who is in the Hall of Fame. At the entrance stands a giant statue of Jim Thorpe, a famous football player who played for the Oorang Indians and other teams in the early 1900s.

From their early gliders to later biplanes, Wilbur (opposite) and Orville Wright made airplanes a reality.

YEAR

1988 An oil tanker spills one million gallons (3.8 million l) of fuel into the Monongahela and Ohio rivers.

EVENT

Ohio has two professional football teams, the Cleveland Browns and the Cincinnati Bengals. The Cleveland Indians and the Cincinnati Reds are the state's professional baseball teams. The Columbus Blue Jackets play hockey, and the Cleveland Cavaliers play basketball.

Adults and children love to watch sports, but there is one sporting event in Ohio in which only children can compete. Every July since 1934 (except during the World War II years of 1941–45), children and teenagers have flocked to Akron for the All-American Soap Box Derby, one of the largest races of its kind in the world. Competitors build their own stock cars and race them on Akron's Derby Downs.

Tourists from around the world come to Ohio to enjoy its cities and countryside. The coast and islands of Lake Erie draw thousands of visitors to northern Ohio each year. Tourists also visit southern Ohio to canoe the Little Miami River or hike through Wayne National Forest.

While Cleveland Browns Stadium (above) is home to the city's football team, its basketball franchise, the Cavaliers (opposite), play at Quicken Loans Arena.

YEAR
1995   The Rock and Roll Hall of Fame opens in Cleveland.
EVENT

- 28 -

QUICK FACTS

While in southern Ohio, many tourists stop at Serpent Mound, one of the largest American Indian mounds in the country. Built by the people known as Mound Builders for religious purposes, the mound dates back to 800 B.C. Visitors can walk along the edge of the snake-shaped mound and take in its mystery.

In Ohio, fishing is an enjoyable pastime for tourists and residents alike. But one river hasn't always been clean enough for fishing. In 1969, the Cuyahoga River near Cleveland was so polluted from factory waste that it caught fire. The fire raised awareness throughout the country about the dangers of pollution. In 1972, the U.S. passed the Clean Water Act. Ohio's rivers and lakes soon became clean again.

Whether one loves the country or the city, in Ohio, either lifestyle is possible. Because of its clean water and growing economy, Ohio continues to draw people to its cities, forests, and waterways. Many will decide to make Ohio their home, and from this prosperous land, more great leaders are sure to come.

YEAR
2003 On August 14, a widespread power outage affects more than three million Ohio residents.
EVENT

BIBLIOGRAPHY

Crawford, Brad. *Compass American Guides: Ohio.* New York: Fodor's, 2005.

Groene, Janet, and Gordon Groene. *Natural Wonders of Ohio: A Guide to Parks, Preserves, and Wild Places.* Castine, Maine: County Roads Press, 1994.

Ohio Historical Society. "Homepage." Ohio Historical Society. http://www.ohiohistory.org.

Wright, David K. *Moon Handbooks: Ohio.* Emeryville, Calif.: Avalon Travel, 2003.

Zimmermann, George, and Carol Zimmermann. *Off the Beaten Path: Ohio.* Guilford, Conn.: Globe Pequot Press, 2005.

INDEX